from the banks
of brook avenue

w r rodriguez

zeugpress

Dedicated to Mike Peterson, in gratitude for his technical advice and support of my publication projects over the decades.

> **Acknowledgments**
>
> Poems from this book previously appeared in the following magazines and anthologies: *And Justice For All; The Bronx County Historical Society Journal; Connections: New York City Bridges in Poetry; Dusty Dog; The Glacier Stopped Here: an anthology of poems by Dane County writers; Live Lines: Is There a Place for Poetry in Your World?; North Coast Review; POETS on the line; The Prose Poem: An International Journal; The Spirit That Moves Us; Tokens: Contemporary Poetry of the Subway; Welcome to Your Life: Writings from the Heart of Young America; You Are Here: New York City Streets in Poetry;* and *Z Miscellaneous*. The short poem, "genghis khan," by w r rodriguez, previously appeared in *Wormwood Review*. It serves as the basis for "yankee kitchen."

Cover Photo: *Glass Clouds* by Rob Rodriguez

© 2015 w r rodriguez
All rights reserved

Printed in the United States of America

ISBN: 978-0-9632201-3-4

zeugpress

Contents

I

forbidden places 7
a moon full and cold 8
just another new york city subway near death experience 10
yankee kitchen 12
the beach beneath the bridge 14
after seeing *night of the living dead* 15
on the coping 16
liberation: the brook avenue parking meter quartet 18
justice 22
she is leaving but 23
what could have more impact than a bus 24
plaza of the undented turtle 26
avenue b, 14th street, looking south 29
the push and break and chase of it 30

II

the third avenue el 33
standing upon the fordham road bridge 37
halloween 38
ne cede malis: poem for the seal of the borough of the bronx 40
washington comes to visit 42
grandfather: a photograph 43
bootblacks on the loose 44
al 46
p.s. 43 47
cypress avenue 50
skully 52
the tire man 54
a small but perfect world 56
the fountain of youth 58

III
welcome to the mainland 61
america's favorite pastime 65
yankee fan 66
the gambling leaguers 69
lost again on old subways 70
randall's island 72
triborough bridge: suspension 75
triborough bridge: stasis 76
triborough bridge: genesis 78
triborough bridge: kinesis 79
astoria park 80
from the banks of brook avenue 82

Bibliography: Previous Publications 84

I

...a wholly new ordering of ordinary affairs.

forbidden places

in all the forbidden places
like round the corner
and too far up the block
and up and down the you'll fall from it fire escape
and across the bad boy bad girl rooftops
of fertile pigeons and antenna thieves

through the sinister shadows of subway stations
and beware of dogs junkies
and the drunken super
basements
through the unexplored side streets of childhood
my mind wanders

that musk of the living
and dying tenement compels me
the gloom of alley and airshaft
the glow of sunlight on brick
i must navigate asphalt rivers
i must trek the broken glass

graffitied mainland to reach
the cement heart of the interior
and i will not return
i am the great explorer forever lost
in the concrete wilderness
i will discover america

flowering in the rubble

a moon full and cold

there was a moon full and cold
and i was a child in the big wide
unwanderable world
kept safe by my parents and warm
while the radiator with its ancient scales
of cracked paint hissed like a tame dragon

through the green forests
and brown fields of footworn linoleum
plastic soldiers advanced from their beachhead
to conquer the living room or to die in glorious battle
cowboys and indians skirmished at fort apache
alien spacecraft landed and robots ran amok

gallant knights with british accents
rode forth from castle walls to great adventure
fighting firebreathing worms and other strange creatures
so the countryside would be safe for travelers
and a child might sleep in bed and fear no harm
there was no gore just valor and victory and i

was general or prince or hero
anything is possible in the moonlight
this is the moon that shone over stalingrad
when death oozed through the rubble
this is the moon that glowed over the balcony
when romeo swore his love and juliet was enchanted

a leafless lifeless moon amid the tarpaper sky
which rose above the rooftops which shrouded our souls
shining white beyond empty streets and unlit windows
beyond unseen sleepers and reason and dream
a moon bright and distant
as a future as a friend as a life beyond the immediate

i pressed my nose to the windowpane and saw the moon
looming over lovers and battlefields
i wanted to sit forever in its light
to drink in the heavens to drown in wonder
ecstatic and enraptured
sated and thirsting for more

the fearless loveless bloodless moon
beyond the who and what and where of the sun's despair
its stark chill beckoned unanswerable

just another new york city subway near death experience

116th street and lexington avenue
three of us in the subway car
like some underground golgotha
when mister death walks in
not looking too kindly
we are not feeling immortal today
he is six feet tall he is five feet wide
he can sit anywhere he wants
but he stands right over me
cold eyes solemn mouth
in one hand a thick belt
dangles like a scythe
(the other holds the commuter strap
for proper balance because giants
do not like to tumble before their prey)
as the train rocks along
like the history of western civilization
which is irrelevant at this moment
of imminent doom
his eyes do not blink
his mouth does not smile
(i have lost my sense of humor
and all other sensation)
that immense hand
that mysterious belt
dangling in my peripheral vision
like a glimpse of heaven beyond pain
i cannot speak
i cannot run
the enormous gray clad arm
moves and the belt
taps my knee
taps my knee three times
his eyes do not move

i do not move
nor think nor feel
i have transcended
humanity in a subway tunnel beneath spanish harlem
and he walks off
to the next passenger
and taps his knee
three times then on to the next
three times and there are only three passengers
so he lumbers into the next car
searching for knees
and i feel like sir gawain released by the green knight
introspective and glad to be alive
i am young and i have learned
that experience is not unique
that the inevitable is
sometimes avoidable though i don't know how
and that for a mere fifteen cent token i can wander
forever searching for the man who taps knees
but when a voice says *shoot boy it was just another*
new york city subway near death experience
i remember that i was going to play basketball and maybe
talk to some girls afterwards though i am
a lousy shot and terribly
socially awkward

yankee kitchen

there are paintings of quaint towns by the sea
and clippers slicing windswept waters
wood trim and white bricks
a touch of new england in new york
with a whiff of chowder on the menu
harbored next to a massive gray church
where angels watch over the world
and the monstrance shines over the globe
and the winged herald on the corner wields a trumpet
louder than all the taxicabs on lexington avenue
if only we could hear it
but we sail the winds and waves of adolescence
and drift back to this modest diner
with its patina of grease and nicotine
to listen to ourselves and feast
upon just being friends
in that delicious time
before the future pulls us apart
and we become like the pedestrians beyond the window
scurrying to love to money to fashionable
restaurants or dive bars
honking like traffic at anything in the way
some of us will make the angels cry
some will just wander off
into life but for now
we have nothing to do but sit
together and sip our sodas until the ice
turns to water while ralph
the aged waiter with the patience of a saint
lean and drawn like the farmer in *american gothic*
and a loving smile pretends not to see
jerry use his straw to shoot spitballs at the good
citizens of nantucket so purposefully
portrayed in oil amid the rustic wooden frame

while in the infernal heat of the kitchen
the anonymous infamous fry cook grills
hamburgers cheeseburgers and anything we can afford
we do not know his name but we call him
genghis khan because legend has it he once
charged from the grill waving a butcher knife
at a customer who complained
so we laugh and to the last
lick of grease eat clean the bone
white plates of our hungry
youth

the beach beneath the bridge

a strip of sand and stone
between overgrown grass and gray water
white suburban homes mottle the leaves
of a distant shore
thirteen years old our footprints
are pools in the mud
we walk away
from parents and baseballs
there are mussels and driftwood
a horizon and a sky
ashes of bonfires burnt out
like the passion of night's lovers
the beach is awash with a love we barely understand
the smell of lowtide mud and brine
there is no going back not yet
the uncertain future ebbs and flows
now beneath the bronx sun we run and laugh
and stumble in the cold dark waves

after seeing *night of the living dead*

stiffarmed we limp across the commons
they're coming to get you barbara
we yell from dormitory bushes
on this hallowed ground
where edgar allan poe
once haunted the jesuits
but no one is scared so we
stagger into the pub to bend
our elbows till dawn
pretending to be
cinema heroes and poets
and in the platonic light of day
when we are only ourselves
they up and run
premeds
junior accountants
student politicians
literally up and run
they conform so well
we not at all
they will flourish and prosper
we will write and paint and teach
and grow old paying bills
starving for the days
and nights when we
roamed the gothic campus
young alive hungry
liberal arts
rebels

on the coping

atop the parapet
of a five story walk-up
on the outer edge
of coping

he stands
fifty feet in the air
upon the smooth
downward slope of tile

his kite soars
a soul
in search of heaven
and he smiles

childhood stops
children gaze
with upturned
wondering eyes

there must be angels
in the clouds
a miracle flutters
overhead

the eternity
of a summer afternoon
the immortality of youth
the timeless awe

those black sneakers
on the brink
of doom
and suddenly

a jump
a blind
backwards leap
onto the tarpaper roof

the kite
sports in the wind
and he descends
creaky stairs

to the rest of his life
to be found years later
jaundiced
needle scarred

dead in the stench
of an unlit doorway

liberation: the brook avenue parking meter quartet

I

the war droned
air america
deathdrugs
slumlord decadence
nightsticks and headblood

nor freedom from ourselves
eternities of tenements
work
sweat
survival

rentstrike
riot
petition
so many nouns and verbs
yet the poor are always among us

II

the resignation
of sun on concrete
the protest wind
of winter apartments
life is the struggle to live

brook avenue is indifferent
to saint and thief
time and space are money
taxation inevitable
and the city will take its tithe

we labor we sleep we dream
we awaken to parking meters
parking meters on brook avenue
where the sewerburied stream flows
invisible as hope

III

where orchards once grew
now stark
silver moneytrees
eat the fruit of our labor
we pay to park and we pay

for the means to make us pay
coinboxes are stolen
and we pay for replacements
by day we spend
by night we are robbed

dime by thin roosevelt dime
from weary hands
our wealth trickles
through treacherous currents
to the ocean of greed

IV

midnight's entrepreneur
is an invisible
lumberjack
hacking a trail of steel stumps
through urban wilderness

a cycle of thievery
and fruitless reforestation
meters reappear
to disappear again
and again and again

and again until
the city withdraws
from this war of attrition
no more parking meters
no more parking meter thief

the avenue is free
as a babbling brook

o liberation

justice

a youth grabbed an old woman's purse fat with tissues and aspirin and such sundries as old women carry in sagging purses a desperate youth nice enough not to beat her head bloody into the sidewalk as muggers of the feeble often do for the fun of it i suppose and he ran up the hill but one of the perennial watchers watched it all from her window the purseless old woman in slow pursuit yelling such curses as it takes old women a lifetime to learn but it was too dangerous too futile the silent watcher knew to call the police who might come and rough up someone they did not like just for the fun of it i suppose or who would talk polite and feel mad inside and roll their eyes because there was really nothing they could do and there were murders and assaults to handle so this silent angry watcher carelessly but carefully dropped flower pots from her fourth floor windowsill garden one crashing before one behind and the third hitting him on the head a geranium i suppose and closed her window while the huffing grateful old woman looked up at the heavens to thank the lord and when she finally calmed down she walked off with her purse laughing and leaving the youth to awaken in the blue arms of the law and do you know two smiling cops walked up all those stairs to warn the watcher that if she weren't more careful with her plants she would get a ticket for littering i suppose

she is leaving but

she is leaving but
pauses a moment
before the great
overhead thud
our upstairs neighbors
like to play so they wrestle
the burly father
the burly son
and the takedown
takes down the ceiling

my amazed aunt had turned to talk
stopped at the french doors
on the threshold of doom
by mundane words
a second before bricks
and whiskey bottles
left by turn of the century
italian plasterers
and genuine plaster
crash in a dusty thud

she laughs to see
a leg poking through
she laughs to be standing
in our living room
an oasis with green sofa and chair
art deco end tables and console television
she laughs just to be alive
in a rent controlled apartment
in the south bronx
where no one escapes death

and she laughs

what could have more impact than a bus

what could have more impact than a bus
boasted the bus on a bus long fluorescent sign
advertising advertising space along the roof
of this new bus and its new bus brethren
who bore the plastic banners of big corporations
making big bucks from this richest
and poorest of cities
but galloping buses are not pedestrians
to be tamed with words and money and this rare
soon to be extinct
what could have more impact than a bus bus
with a bellyful of passengers and its fluorescent plastic strip
sped past the bright shops and dark taverns
along third avenue where once
the great sad eyed el roared
and rattled tenement windows
and this rare soon to be extinct
what could have more impact than a bus bus
right outside the seventy-sixth street flophouse
where nightly floppers staggered home
amid swinging staggering singles
in the very crosswalk where daily the ancient monsignor
damn near ran out of breath while we wondered
how long he had left how many months or minutes
until he could no longer hobble to safety
before the light turned and he would be caught
in the stampede of uptown traffic and be killed
while we watched like the crowd at calvary
and did nothing to save him
we would carry the guilt to our graves
we would suffer gruesome memories
we would sweat through grisly nightmares
but he died quietly in his sleep
and the angels carried him away

and we were just streetcorner losers
with time to kill
then one day this rare soon to be extinct
what could have more impact than a bus bus
caught in mid escape a white pigeon
white as a baptismal gown white as a stained
glass window dove on a sunny sunday morning
a rare aberration of the prolific pigeons
those fellow gray loiterers
whose droppings whitewashed the steeples
of the church that spiked its windowsills
and swept up wedding rice before the flock could partake
a rare white winged apparition
caught like any of us might have been
by this rare soon to be extinct
what could have more impact than a bus bus
and it fell wide eyed
its feathers drifting slowly
spiraling white and red onto the asphalt
ground down by car after car until
even the blood disappeared
and the flying spirit disintegrated into the busy world
outside the dive bar beneath the flophouse
that will die and be reborn
in a paradise of condominiums and upscale cafes
with no room for the congregation
the aged priest may have been trying to save
with no room for elevated trains
or bored teenage boys
there was prophecy and revelation and the promise
of eternity and we knew
we too might grow old someday
if we were that lucky

plaza of the undented turtle

sirens
red lights
angry cops
the gold car speeds
down avenue
c and swerves
onto the sidewalk
through the plaza
scattering
the twelfth street midnight
beer drinkers and slams
head-on into the shell
of the beloved
cement turtle
while the skyline sparkles
postcard pretty
outside our window
ten stories above
as we watch this drama
just another city night
just another summer street
just another urban legend
seeking anonymity
reality entertains
when it happens to others and
the door flies open
the foot race begins
run driver run
from police
run police run
into the night
flow river flow
to the mysterious sea
who knows

how it ends
is there justice
on dark streets
red lights gather and vanish
gather and vanish
all life long
blood bleeds
bullets kill
the turtle
does not cry
the pontiac
has chosen to remain silent
then the impounding officer
starts the engine
it purrs it revs and it's off
to automobile prison
there is no reporter
asking the cop at the wheel
about inanimate
reincarnation
it really does
have a phoenix
painted on the hood
there is irony
to fulfill
tragedy
lust
love and laughter
babies will surface from the womb
to crawl to walk to climb
searching
for the ecstasy of heaven
now the undented turtle sleeps
beneath the electric hum

of the power plant which may
or may not explode
with a hiss and a fireball
and a boom like the big bang
as if the universe were created anew
on the lower east side
and we are lucky just to breathe
amid the smoke and the screams
and we are lucky to survive
the chaos of night
and the turtle waits for the warm sun
for the silly day for the children
to play like creatures
on the back
of the great
creator
god

avenue b, 14th street, looking south

there is a place when
there is a moment where
crossing the street
all the streetlights stretching south
and all the traffic lights
align in rows
that would converge but for
some distant building
and i think i must be
exactly in the middle
of the street but i know
the world is too crooked
for that

the push and break and chase of it

three men push a broken car down the street.
a dog chases them.

three dogs push a broken man down the street.
a car chases them.

three cars push a broken dog down the street.
a man chases them.

three men, three cars, three dogs
push each other down the street,
chase each other,
break each other.

no, no, we must not upset the order,
said the car who was really three cars who had chased the dogs.

a little innovation is in order every now and then,
said the man who was really three men who had chased the cars.

do we not constitute a microcosm of the universal flux
from order to disorder to the establishment of a new order
to be set to chaos?
said the dog who was really three dogs who had chased the men
and who now chased cars
following a wholly new ordering
of ordinary
affairs.

II

...our spirits drink immortal rage and compassion from the fluorescent green ooze of the waterbug writhing fountain of youth

the third avenue el

I. 1886

a bridge and shining rails span the river
the long arm of the el stretches north
from harlem through the mainland
the seeds of the bronx are sown
tenements will blossom on fertile ground
there will be streets and streetcars and immigrants

will brave the broad ocean for their chance
in the land of the free
the colossus rises above new york harbor
glorious timeless stoic
her mighty limb bears a beacon of hope
a wary welcome to the new world

where geronimo is imprisoned
where chinese laborers are expelled from seattle
where former slaves are massacred in a mississippi courthouse
no one is indicted for their murder
in this great republic where the lord
and manifest destiny work in mysterious ways

a torch a tablet a stern look
staring toward the tempestuous atlantic
the copper matron will guide
exiles to the promised land
sure footed she is stepping
in the direction of south ferry station

II. 1920

from the battery park aquarium
to the botanical gardens and beyond
all for a buffalo nickel
a stadium will be built and there will be baseball
in the bronx and babe ruth and the yankees
will come and the crowds will cheer

in the golden age when the poor
inherit the earth one apartment at a time
the multitudes have arrived a new world is rising
farms become tenements
immigrants become americans
who will rest who will eat who will work

who will raise families and ride that great train
to a modest job and home to a modest kitchen
commuters flicker past trackside windows
curtains flutter and the glass shakes
garlic and cabbage and old country recipes
simmer on the flames of freedom

green stanchions green stations
lady liberty has turned green above the gray water
the sidewalks are gray the tenements are brown
or white or gray or red and the street gets little sunlight
children play and laugh in the shadows
the el sparks and thunders and storms across the sky

III. 1955

the sons and daughters of immigrants
survived poverty and prohibition
the depression and two world wars
now their children are given dog tags
and schools teach to duck and cover
when atomic bombs explode

but the economy is booming
the city thrives and factories flourish
televisions toys cars
disneyland gunsmoke the mickey mouse club
mcdonald's opens in illinois and eisenhower
sends aid and advisors to vietnam

this humble train this noble artery of democracy
the bronx harlem yorkville
lenox hill murray hill
little italy and chinatown
in this land where liberty proudly enlightens the world
rosa parks is arrested and the boycott begins

the third avenue el is mortal it lives it moves
it dies a long slow death
the aquarium has been closed and the fish deported
ellis island is abandoned to rot in the harbor
on the final manhattan run people doff their hats
and toast the last echoes of its passing glory

IV. 1973

the once great el is merely
a minor shuttle an appendix
lost in the intestines of the bronx
the dodgers and giants have migrated west
the yankees wane and rust
mottles the rivets of industry

america the beautiful wrestles with itself
broken glass lost dreams
riots and assassinations
planned obsolescence and withdrawal with honor
the weary el clatters like a faithful milk wagon
while tenements crumble and die

the world trade center rises above the skyline
the last passenger run is made in the dark
and the train disappears in the night
the streets will be quiet and sidewalks
freed from shadow but the world
will not seem so wonderful

towers will rise where towers have fallen
the bronx will rise from the ruin
ellis island will reopen and the children
of the children of immigrants will come
to behold that great green lady
her colossal foot trampling forever the broken chain of slavery

her torch pointing to heaven
where stars are innumerable stations

and the great train rumbles toward paradise

standing upon the fordham road bridge

on a walk from nothing to do to nowhere to go
i stop here beneath heaven and above the harlem
river which curves from spuyten duyvil to hell gate
past the train yard and bus barn and power plant
through bluffs of tenement and project
in a valley veiled in concrete and night

all those little people with their big lives
all those big people with their little lives
asleep now or wandering the streets
searching for a cool breeze in the humid gloom
or cheap or expensive thrills which bring
forgetfulness of whatever pain there is to life

and i have found the river
darker and deeper it seems than space itself
though the sky is a gray haze of city light
which obscures the stars as we are obscured
and i stand above unheard currents
where tall masted ships no longer sail

i watch striations of light on the midnight water
which casts no human reflection
and tells no tales of what it carries away
the silent inscrutable current is a thirst
to be salted by unfathomable oceans
and in the depth of this drowning darkness

the faint vision of dawn
bringing a new day to this weary world

halloween

detroit burns and the bronx is mugged
with socks full of stones the wicked beat
money from mortal flesh
pirates and devils
torment candy from the naive

riots and thievery and war always war
there are no loving arms
strong enough to fend off the world
blood and grief and bloated bodies
children starve and the innocent die but tonight

the slaughtered will rise from sprawling graves
tonight urchins will drift across mine fields
their ghostly songs whine like artillery
and in mockery eggs splatter
like bombs from unseen rooftops

o do wear a mask of a monster or mutant
it is less hideous than to look
helpless into the face of humanity
there were saints and gods among us
and we killed them

blessed are the dead who have been purged
of cruelty and greed
they know what we have lost
forlorn paradise heaven uncreated
they know and they will come

the intentionally killed the merely neglected
they who should fear but who love nevertheless
they will come who have been liberated
from the perpetual procreation of pain and stolen joy
they will come and they will dance

look look their bliss wafts through the tangible
we smile and we pray that the children will be safe
let us feed the darling monsters coin and corn
we who are so generous and who will send yet more
souls suffering to their graves for our great blessing

ne cede malis: **poem for the seal of the borough of the bronx**

yield not to evil
meet misfortune boldly
wings spread
head cocked
beak in profile
one stern
alert eye
stares forth
the bald eagle is perched
atop the hemisphere
the stylized cupule
of an acorn
a triangular shield
where the sky is broken
by the straight beams
of a circular sun
whose indifferent eyes
surface over calm water
peace and liberty shining
on the ripples of commerce
and at the base
a small triangle
dark
almost insignificant
it is the land
of new hope and old tradition
behold it is the bronx
here unseen millions create their lives
and await their fate
in the scroll
the ominous motto
ne cede malis
yield not to evil
all is surrounded

by a festooned circle
a suggestion of universal harmony
the sun has eyebrows
it is all so placid
the sky is cloudless
the waters still
the land a mere shoreline
a speck in eternity
and the eagle
watches his back
a wary carnivore
in a troublesome world

washington comes to visit

he arrives at grandma's house
just off cypress avenue
but nana does not serve him a bowl of her soup
and poppop does not offer him a hand-rolled cigar
and dad does not take his picture
because they are not home
it is 1781 and even their home is not there
but the british are
and washington is scouting enemy positions
so the redcoats welcome him
with cannon fire
from harlem and randall's island and nearby ships
but the general
continues his visit and goes
to the shoe shine parlor on brook avenue
uncle al does not give him a free shine
mom and aunt jean are not standing in the doorway
aunt helen is not watching from her window
and grandfather does not run out
into 138th street as he does
to welcome roosevelt's motorcade
he shines the cops' shoes
so they let him shake
the hand of the beloved f.d.r.
but washington is not yet president
and the shoe shine parlor and 138th street
and cypress avenue and brook avenue are not there
though the millbrook is and so is the mill
and muskets fire and cannons roar
it is noisy as the fourth of july
and washington plans to attack manhattan
and bring peace and quiet to the neighborhood
but he marches to yorktown instead
and the rest is history

grandfather: a photograph

standing outside
the shoe shine parlor
a short man
in a long apron
brushes in hand
elbows bent
a gray face
an impatient smile
as if to say
hurry
take the picture
there is work to do
my customers are waiting

bootblacks on the loose

we are bootblacks on the loose
and we might be found
in jersey or north of the county line
on summer tuesdays we swim
at palisades amusement park
the world's largest salt water pool
we cling to the board beneath the waterfall
and lose ourselves in the briny roar
saturday night it's pepper steak
at a chinese restaurant in yonkers
or a burger at ho jo's
where uncle al tries to convince
the waitress that i am an unusually short thirty-one year old
looking for a date
thought i am thirteen and still wrestling with puberty
sunday afternoon it might be
the bowling alley by yankee stadium
or the billiard parlor on brook avenue
cousin billy is gifted with great strength
and an abundance of enthusiasm
he subdues the pins with brute force
he breaks the rack with a thunderbolt
scaring the balls into pockets
and he pounds the leather into a shine
while sandy finesses his strikes and sweet talks
the bank shots and coaxes the shoes
to perfection
i suck at everything but have fun anyway
i am learning to sweat my way through a shine
not the strongest
not the suavest
but i get the job done
i cannot outswim
uncle al though billy

can beat him at bowling
and sandy can beat him at pool
but al's arms are like tree trunks
he has been a bootblack
longer than the three of us have been alive
and no pair of shoes
can make him sweat
he loves to take us places
when we are not working
and to play gin rummy when it rains
and to lie in the sun
on the boardwalk at palisades
and smoke a cigar after lunch
while we wait
so we won't get cramps
the proper amount of time
between eating and swimming
is exactly how long it takes
for al to finish his cigar
so we watch the manhattan skyline
and boats on the hudson river
and women in bikinis
and we wish
the day would never end

al

his father was a bootblack
and he is a bootblack
shining shoes with graceful movements
a faint smile beneath his moustache
while big band music plays on the ancient radio

and when the brushes dance
over the leather he leans
slightly like a man
gently holding the waist of a woman
in a prohibition era ballroom

p.s. 43

jonas bronck elementary school
he settled in paradise
on the east bank of the harlem river
divinely guided to a virgin forest
of unlimited opportunity
that needed only an industrious hand
to make it the most beautiful
region in the world he claimed
but we grew up on streets without trees
and we gathered in the auditorium to watch
space flights on a black and white television
the stage had a mural
of the purchase of the bronx
guys in tight black suits and long white stockings
and some sachem outside a longhouse
the suits were not spandex
and the longhouse was not made
of barclay-barclite fiberglass panels
and just beyond the panorama
maybe some old lenape was saying
there goes the neighborhood
they are letting the whites in
they do not even speak the language
is that real money or are these guys just
a couple of broke tulip farmers with counterfeit wampum
when a launch was delayed we watched reruns
of *my little margie*
then it was back to the space race
because america must beat russia to the moon
so the commies would not invade the bronx
and we stockpiled tanks and troops in europe
and we saved the world for democracy
though we could not save the neighborhood
from drugs and crime

and in our kindergarten classroom
midnight vandals threw the teacher's coffee into the aquarium
the goldfish was floating belly up in the morning
no one talked us through our sadness and fear
it was a tough school
if you barfed in the cafeteria you had to clean it up yourself
which led to more barfing
you cleaned and barfed till you barfed no more
and there was nothing more to clean
then you went to class or went home
my mother had her own memories
of this educational institution
where teachers put clothes hangers
inside kids' shirts to encourage good posture
and criticized mom because her parents spoke italian
and not good english
so when they sent letters home in spanish
which neither she nor i could read
she shared her disgruntlement at the main office
but the next letter came again in spanish
and she returned again and again
she was quite good at expressing disgruntlement
in perfect bronx english
most of us were not bilingual but we were quick learners
in kindergarten we were not taught the alphabet
but the first grade teacher assumed we knew it
we learned this is the way life would always be
full of irony and incongruity and strange paintings
and of love and disgruntlement and rebellion
in third grade i became enamored
with a leopard skin coat
there was a redhead inside it
i don't remember her name
but what a coat

when they painted the doors pink
and put a DO NOT TOUCH sign on the wall
how could i resist
shoving my hat into the wet paint
they would not arrest me for it
they would not send me to the principal
the redhead would not be impressed
even my mother would not yell
at something so absurd
it was like the rich taking money from the poor
it was like going to the moon while the world was dying
it was like sending troops to vietnam
it was like arsonists burning tenements
even when the slumlords did not pay them
it was like writing poetry
instead of working on wall street
it was like jonas settling the bronx
and thinking he could improve paradise
it was because there was a sign
saying not to
it was because the tenements
were crumbling and the trees had vanished
and john wayne had killed all the indians
except for a few token sidekicks
it was because
it was there
and i had a hat
and the paint was wet
and i was a stupid kid
with a pink hat
receiving a great education
in america

cypress avenue

the avenue is named for the trees
that once grew in the morris arboretum
before the age of development and ruin
they are gone but their spirits linger
on this quiet avenue in the noisy bronx
a half mile of peace and simple wonder
or is it just childhood illusion
the thrill of saint mary's park
the lure of the randall's island walkway
the corner candy store
that sells joyva halvah and joyva joys
chocolate covered raspberry jelly bars
so tart and sweet even hamlet
would find succulence in the dull world
at grandmother's apartment her cooking
brightens the railroad flat
the aroma seeps out the window
and the street seems to sparkle
there is a green beauty salon
a turquoise shoe shine parlor
p.s. 65 with its light brown bricks
sparrows chirp in the schoolyard
and when the basketball courts are deserted
in the solitude of a sunday afternoon
even a clumsy kid
can pretend to be an all-star
the millbrook housing projects
are young and pink
christmas lights blink in various windows
i watch the flashing colors
to the point of insanity
while daddy warms up his 54 plymouth
in an outdoor parking lot by a scraggly locust tree sapling
as the car radio plays

wonderland by night
and i wonder
about the abandoned public school
p.s. 29 is bone white in the harsh sun
a spectral glow in the dark
the children say it is haunted
and i am a child
and in a long narrow store
lost in the red and yellow flames
of arson perhaps
father buys me the black knight of nurnberg
it is the missing piece
of my collection of aurora plastic models
the red knight of vienna
the blue knight of milan
the silver knight of augsberg
there is a gold knight of nice
i do not know it exists but it would be nice to have
i would lust for it as i did for the black knight
but my temporal desires have been temporarily satisfied
i am happy for a while
and safe for a while
in bed at night surrounded
by stuffed animals that protect me from bad dreams
while the knights keep watch from my shelves
there are tears and joy
there are more things to fear in heaven and earth
than i can dream of
as i glue together the armor
that protects me from the world

skully

we squat we crawl we kneel
we lie on the sidewalk to shoot
bottle caps from square to square
in a game that demands
intimate contact with the street
and we play it with a summer frenzy
on a worn slab of cement outside 514
smooth almost as hallway marble
the only one like it on the block
in the neighborhood in the known world
unmarred by cracks and even
the residue of long discarded chewing gum
has become one with the surface
a man-made stone made perfect by time
and we study the board with the intensity
of pool hall hustlers and we flick
the middle finger off the thumb
make the shot and go again
hit an opponent and advance
we grow calluses on fingers and palms
we wear holes in dungarees years before
it becomes fashionable
our knees blacken but we do not care about arthritis
and we do not care how stiff the iron-on patches feel
before we wear holes in them too
our mothers mend and sew
our fathers say
who do you think i am rockefeller
when we ask for a dime to buy soda
so we do not ask for new pants
they were children of the great depression
they are hard working men and if there is change
in their pockets we will get that orange nehi
and we will save the cap and fill it

with melted crayons and we will line up
and shoot away the summer afternoon
angling from square to square
one to four on each corner
five through twelve midway on each side
thirteen in the center
again and again we crisscross deadman's zone
and must avoid disaster
like our fathers went from poverty to war to the thankless jobs
they are grateful to have
like the big boys flirt
with drugs police crime paternity
they hope to get out of adolescence alive
and survive their unknown futures
there is a wall around berlin
the russians are building missile bases in cuba
and vietnam looms beyond the sunset of many childhoods
the line between victory and defeat is chalk thin
we must make that crucial shot
into the thirteenth box
dead center in deadman's zone
and live to tell about it

the tire man

nixon is rising and the yankees are falling
and i am walking to my political science class
i walk up the hill and down the hill
and a long way along fordham road
in my adolescent oblivion
and i stop
when a tire rolls across the sidewalk
i do not drive but i am a good pedestrian
i yield to rolling tires
even those not attached to cars
another tire follows it
and another
i see a tire lying on the ground
and the man in the back of a truck
drops a tire straight down so it hits
in just the right spot and rolls
across the sidewalk and up the ramp
to be caught and loaded onto the dock
they do not teach this in college so i watch
i cannot explain the vectors involved nor the probability
of repeatedly dropping a tire onto the exact spot
to give it sufficient momentum and an accurate path
i left the engineering program to become an english major
so the poetic beauty of it is enough for me
there are a few sliders and curves but the tires
always get to where they are going
and when the show is over i go to class
where tests are being returned and the professor says
i gave you 35 points for putting your name on the paper
because it is good to know your name
so how can one of you get a 42
i do not know who got the bad score
and i do not know the name
of the tire man

just another nondescript earning an honest living
he will never run for president
he will never pitch for the yankees
but there are no spitballs
and he throws a perfect game

a small but perfect world

at thanksgiving we give thanks
for all we take for granted
the turkey the lasagne
the ceiling over our head
our apartment in the south bronx
the bedrooms are small
the dining room is not
we gather and feast
and the table is cleared
soon construction begins
the plywood is covered in a green grass mat
tracks are laid out and screwed down and wired up
engines and cars are placed on the rails for a test run
then the landscape is made complete
a city hall a bank a hospital
suburban townhouses
a farmhouse a barn and pens for the livestock
cows and pigs and chickens and trees
little people sitting on benches
at the station or on lounge chairs
at the little motel or in a suburban backyard
or walking to the diner or to the mailbox
or waving lanterns beside switch towers
there are platforms for the unloading
of milk cans and logs
a radar tower and a light tower
a water tank and crossing signals
these are the toys my parents never had
during the depression
now dad works in the financial district
where the buildings are tall and the streets are narrow
crowded by day and deserted by night
and before the world trade center
there are clearing houses and discount shops

so the bargains come home
the landscape is filled in
and expanded to the tall buffet
connected to the lowlands by mountains
which mom makes by painting grocery bags
and crumpling them and shaping them
a beautiful illusion in the heart of reality
a small but perfect world
where the streets are clean
and nobody gets mugged on the way to the store
where no one sets buildings on fire
or dies of an overdose in a back alley doorway
it is like living in the land of *leave it to beaver*
a small but perfect world
where there is much to be thankful for
christmas comes and the new year is celebrated
then each illusion is put back into its box
and the dining room table
is again just the dining room table
and school reopens
the cold of january sets in
and we are
still
thankful

the fountain of youth

the sewer backed up and the street filled with glowing green water which all began when a neighborhood juvenile delinquent who was not very neighborly and who robbed from friend and foe alike like he just did not care lifted the manhole cover to show us the sights so we gathered to watch in awe brown walls of waterbugs writhing like times square on new year's eve and a few leapt up into daylight and into our nightmares for these were the winged tanks of the cockroach army whose armor mere sneakers could not destroy and we jumped back squealing and laughing then but not later and this neighborhood juvenile delinquent who was not very neighborly and who robbed from friend and foe alike like he just did not care liked to impress us so he threw seven milk crates perfectly suitable for sitting down the shaft but no one would sit in the street that hot summer night to talk and to watch the kids play punchball in the dark and there would be no open air games of dominoes or poker because the sewer backed up so much that the city sent a crew to repair it while we stood in the doorways to watch the strange sight of something actually getting fixed but things get worse before they get better the old timers always say and the maintenance crew flooded the sewer with dye which went down and came up and the waterbugs went down and the milk crates came up and the street filled with glowing green water which the maintenance men left like they just did not care so for a week no one played outside and the neighborhood juvenile delinquent hung out somewhere else and the shoppers and the commuters walked next to the buildings to avoid the chartreuse stench which took so long to recede that it became the evergreen symbol of what the city thought of us like it just did not care and of how we could not play on our own street which we would never forget though someday we might get lucky and hit the number or write a hit tune and move someplace where glowing green water would never happen somewhere like fifth avenue or sutton place where our bodies grow old and fat while our spirits drink immortal rage and compassion from the fluorescent green ooze of the waterbug writhing fountain of youth

III

...on the banks of brook avenue
where childhood is idyllic
and the world could not be more beautiful

welcome to the mainland

stagger from the atlantic's swell
seek land legs on ellis island
floundering through bureaucracy
and ferried to narrow streets awash
with humanity on the golden shores
of lower manhattan

the brooklyn bridge is a masterpiece
a magnificent temptation
but that alluring long island
stretches east and disintegrates
it points back to the world
you sailed so long to leave

now you migrate north
your ship has come and it has left
you tired and poor
yearning masses huddled and tossed
by the rattle and rock of the train
metal wheel upon metal rail

grinding and sparking
through the wonders of the city
beyond hell gate to paradise
where the tenements are young
where freedom is a peninsula
with heat and indoor plumbing

the brakes squeal the doors
to the new world open
welcome to the mainland welcome
to the bronx where all seems possible
here subways whoosh
underground and roar through the sky

there are rooms for rent
there is always room for one more
friend relative countryman
for one more lost soul
for one more exile
and the horizon fills with brick and glass

behind every silver window lies a dream
which may or may not be fulfilled
and in the cold snuggling of dark winter
or the wriggling of humid summer nights
babies are conceived and they are born
in america

this is not the land of your birth
though the native tongue remains
and the food tastes familiar
at dinner time that old world aroma
wafts through the hallway
the clatter of pots and pans

reverberates in the air shaft
where clotheslines sag with laundry
readied for the great
assimilation of work and school
backyard and alley echo
with multilingual profanity

prayers rise to the heavens
there are churches and synagogues
street corner preachers
rooms where idealists
contemplate utopia and the right
to believe or not to believe

there are times of prosperity
times of common despair
and always the children play
on sandlot and side street
in park and playground
they sing and cry and taunt and cheer

there are saloons and speakeasies
and saloons once again
ice cream parlors and candy stores
vaudeville and movies
all manner of entertainment
under the sun and under the moon

war will come and peace will come
again and again and there will be
parades and memorials and protests
you will grow old and remember
those days of struggle and joy
those friends relatives neighbors

lost in a changing world
where streets disappear and housing projects
spring forth like towers of babel
belgian blocks and trolley tracks
drown in rivers of asphalt
and moses parts the land

his great road cleaves its heart
there is exodus
poverty turmoil and tragedy
tenements burn and fall
there is rubble and more rubble
anger and desperation

ash and dust and broken bricks
and a spirit that suffers but does not die
and a hope that emerges
like weeds from the ruin
the survivors will fight
and new americans will come

the void will fill
with townhouses and pocket parks
there will be new music
new art and new words
and the aroma of exotic foods
will waft through the streets

fragrant and pungent
hopeful

and free

america's favorite pastime

and so it came to pass that the shortest kid in ninth grade was tired of the tallest kid in ninth grade not tired of the vertical difference but just tired of being pushed around so one bright sunny bronx morning the short kid came with a baseball bat and chased the tall kid around the schoolyard until the teachers took the bat and sent us all to class in this melting pot school where we did not quite fit the recipe so the bureaucracy batted us around and threw us curveballs like having us retake the reading test because our scores were too high and declaring 85 the passing grade and decimating our academically advanced class of those with hispanic surnames or dark skin but maybe this was still better than last year in that other school where gangs beat up anyone who was not violent like that quiet little spanish girl who ran crying and screaming down the hallway after the principal came into the classroom and announced the names of kids who were being kicked out of the program and being sent back to eighth grade in their respective ghetto schools but what did the principal care she was just a little girl from some other neighborhood and this is america this is social darwinism this is junior high school where only the strong survive like that short kid with the baseball bat that they took away but they could not stop him and after school he took out a baseball from his pocket and chased the tall kid all the way to the train station and is it not america's favorite pastime to watch big guys beating on little guys and little guys beating on big guys while spectators laugh and cheer glad they are not getting beat up and just hoping to survive

yankee fan

my cap is navy blue and boldly embroidered
with white interlocking letters
i bought it in my old neighborhood in the bronx
five bucks at a store on creston avenue
a converted newsstand that sells
handbags trinkets statues umbrellas
everything but candy and newspapers
yes the kids and i have inherited
my mother's love for a good bargain
and her loyalty to the home team
but the yankees are always on the road when we visit
so we cruise dollar stores and discount joints
and watch the game on television
and watch grandma watching the game
rooting for hits and home runs
putting whammies on opposing pitchers
screaming with the intensity
of a green bay packers fan when the bears are losing
and i wear my new york yankees baseball cap
all over madison wisconsin
where everyone is so politically correct
and motivated by humanitarianism or legislation
taught from childhood not to hurt anyone's feelings
and these friendly and sensitive midwesterners
are compelled to say hello to passersby
even those wearing new york yankee caps
but like some landlocked progeny
of the ancient mariner they must catch my eye
and tell me with compulsive conviction
that they hate the yankees
and i must smile and listen
to these hardworking middle americans
as they denounce good old american capitalism
at least as it applies to winning teams

but i am too polite to tell them
i mostly wear the cap to keep the sun out of my eyes
though i do have some recall
of kubek boyer and richardson
and an aging mantle hitting a home run
three balls two strikes two outs
in the bottom of the ninth *holy cow*
and mel stottlemyre's inside-the-park grand slam
but i was too young to understand the game
and when i was old enough to appreciate baseball
the yanks were so bad they had rocky colavito pitch
and the best catch i saw at the stadium
was made by a fat i mean overweight
i mean corporally-gifted woman
she had a straw hat three feet in diameter
and when the foul ball bounced off a box seat rail
she held up her hat and it went right in
she might have been from the midwest
or the grand concourse and who knows
where she bought that oversized beach hat
and that magnificent muumuu
the fans applauded the beauty of it
finally something to cheer about
and the right field grandstand
gave her a standing ovation
we wanted to offer her a contract
she was built like the bambino
and we needed a new superstar
instead we got a decade of despair
but how can i explain this to those who are compelled
to tell me that they hate the yankees
while i am compelled to listen
i who was raised in the era
before lawyers and psychologists and sensitivity training

raised in an environment so insensitive
it invented the bronx cheer
i who do not hate the cubs or the brewers
though i will not watch the braves
after all those america's team commercials
because this is america and no american
should be told who to root for
and that smiley faced cleveland indians' logo
is too offensive even for my politically incorrect taste
but i do not explain this
it would take too long and these friendly
fellow americans might ask
about my brooklyn accent
even though i am from the bronx
just like the yankees so i let them talk
and when their strange power of speech
is done and they are once again
congenial madisonians
i simply reply
the more you hate us the more we love it
the more you boo us the more fun it is to win

the gambling leaguers

cheer of crowd crack of bat slap of leather
what beauty in the grace of the great
in the arc of arm of ball of leaping body
the skillful passion of these sandlot ballers
these gambling leaguers these seasonal warriors
waging serious sport in parks and playgrounds
on diamonds of clay or asphalt
against a background of bridge and school
of factory and tenement
a colorful panorama of the ordinary
no one asks for autographs
just victory over the tedium of work and bills
and the urban summer's ceaseless heat
this childhood game fought with adult intensity
for stakes of fifty or a hundred per position or more
side bets among spectators and the excitement begins
the fans live and die in suspense
the winners are rich the losers poor
celebration and frustration and the promise
of the next game the next season
so they play till the money runs out
till legs no longer run till arms no longer throw
with the speed and strength of youth and they fade
into the bleachers to wait
to play again perhaps
where summer is eternal
and the umpires
omniscient

lost again on old subways

i am lost again on old subways
at third avenue station the lights go out
the lunatic laughs
the lunatic who does not appear
until the lights go out
and i cannot see him
and i cannot see what he is laughing at
he laughs and he laughs
death is solemn
but suffering is hysterical
when it happens to others
the three fates the three stooges
torturing each other while the children laugh
until the lights go out and they are stuck
in their own nightmares
and he laughs at my fear
and i laugh at him laughing at my fear
because i am afraid not to
keep the lunatic happy
i have paid my fare and i must journey
there is nowhere to go but where the darkness takes me
and i must get my money's worth
the doors will not open
i cannot depart at the home station
and i slip past my sleeping parents
under the bronx and over the bronx
all the unseen passengers on this runaway train
are laughing and laughing
because we are afraid to stop
we are lost in the bronx
where guns will not save us
and the churches are closed for the night
and the candles lit for the souls of the dead
have burned out and the priests

have locked the rectories
and we are laughing too hard to pray
and we are laughing so hard we almost enjoy it
we have transformed we are the laughing commuters
of the IRT which never looked so good
though we cannot see it as it trembles on
through the night which does not stop
through strange territories where strangers lurk
in the shadows waiting for a few laughs

randall's island

I

here the sky is blue and the water dark
and the bronx an invisible memory
here clouds roll off the continent
goodbye goodbye go rain upon the old world
should it still exist

here the new city greets ancient tides
at the corner of harlem and hell gate
and distinctions obscure
where is the end where is the beginning
how many have drowned like names in the wind

chaotic currents chaotic streets
the orderly megalithic shoreline
of a fishdead metropolis
a horizontal stonehenge on which to celebrate
existence and the rats seem to dance

i cast my bait into the emptiness
launch my kite to the sun
no fish to catch no one to meet
this is a forgotten island
obscure as childhood

II

the confluence of memory and dream
this prehistoric erosion from the mainland
a muddle of time and amazing eternity
there are moments when dandelions roar
in sunlight like british muskets

when summer grass shimmers
as if the present were luminous
while churning and dark the currents
muffle all sound and the unheard
skyline rises to the unspeaking heavens

the delinquent cursed at toil and at play
the institutionalized soul
screamed with rage and frustration
in the infants' hospital the foundling cried
and succumbed to quiet death

the house of refuge the idiot asylum the orphanage
razed and forgotten
and the triborough bridge rises
above park and playground and stadium
amid the wayward whispers of these outcast lands

III

green ticket booths and silver railings
the bleachers are empty and in the plaza
the bronze discus thrower stands naked and alone
trimmed hedges low walls red brick
i balance between fantasy and failure

beneath the pillars of the viaduct
i learn my clumsy insignificance
this is a sacred place and we bury
songless parakeets in shoe boxes after they die
and launch plastic rockets to the virgin moon

between fact and delusion the line has vanished
the little hell gate has drowned in the garbage landfill
the bridge to the psychiatric hospital
stands irrelevant over a river of grass
and rabbits run mad across evening fields

what insane dreams wander the wasteland
darkness drizzles and night
awakens the restless tenements
wisps of arson smog the horizon and i must return
i must and it seems

even i am not here

triborough bridge: suspension

    the

    sky

    road rises

    quickly above green

    shores and gray waters

from astoria to wards island from anchorage to massive anchorage

    graceful cables curve

    sturdy

    blue

    arches

    crowned

    with art deco lanterns

atop steel towers that aspire to heaven above the turbulent hell gate

    bearing the stress of humanity

    festooning the night

    with man

    made

    stars

triborough bridge: stasis

where is everybody going
the best part of this bridge is the middle
between here and there
between above and below
between all the points
on the invisible compass
of our existence
between scylla and charybdis
to the east the solemn frown
of the railroad bridge over the bucolic hell gate
to the west the land of opportunity and misfortune
the magnificent skyline
a forest of penthouse and project
where the homeless home in the shadows
humanity is beautiful from a distance
the landfills bloom with green growth
frivolous waves drown the effluence
of the money mad world
to the north the sewage treatment plant
that will never make us clean
and the manhattan psychiatric hospital
and the center for the criminally insane
and the abandoned asylum
where inmates laughed at pedestrians
as they walked across the sky
in the longago days of carefree strolls
before random violence
before muggings in broad daylight
the happy people of wards island
picnic beneath trees
to the south children splash
in the clear blue water of astoria pool
imagining that they are sharks
or whales or submarines

imagining that summer will never end
reality is such an imposition
like the grim stone of the war memorial
just beyond their youthful laughter
and above restless clouds drive by
on their ceaseless commute
below there is bedlam and mayhem and the tides
swirl over suicides and shipwrecks
but here in the middle there is peace
there is stasis
there is the music
of wind murmuring through cables
why must every polluted river be crossed
here words are invisible
and the past is no more
the future is but the loss of the present
leap to the sky
not to fly
jump to the water
never to swim again
walk ashore
to live and die in the eternal city
where the meek await to inherit
what is left of the earth
o the hovering the hovering

triborough bridge: genesis

in the beginning there was the land and the water
the water separated the mainland from the islands
and moses said *may there be a great bridge*
to join the islands to the islands and the islands to the mainland
it was good and moses said
may there be roads and highways that lead to the great bridge
that joins the islands to the islands and the islands to the mainland
it was good and moses said
may there be parks and playgrounds
for the people in the cars that drive
on the roads and highways that lead to the great bridge
that joins the islands to the islands and the islands to mainland
it was good and moses said
may there be money to build the great bridge
and the roads and highways and parks and playgrounds
and behold there was money
the nation went to work and it was good
the steel industry lit its furnaces and factories reopened
loggers logged and sawmills sawed
railroads hauled lumber across the continent
laborers constructed wooden forms and poured cement
barges ferried girders over the water and towers rose
cables were wound and anchored
the deck suspended and the roadway paved
the great bridge joined the islands to the islands
and the islands to the mainland
there were parks and parkways and the president
came for the opening ceremony
and the people came and rushed to be first
to pay the toll and cross the great bridge
and more people came to pay the toll
more people and more money
money that could be used to build more bridges
and it was all good
but moses did not rest

triborough bridge: kinesis

an automobile vortex
where three bridges meet
twelve directions of traffic
twenty-two lanes that do not intersect
cars can go from here to there to another there
this is america and there are tolls
to pay and toll booths to collect the money
and police to collect those who do not pay the toll
but we kids are oblivious to the wonders of engineering
and we have no money to give to trolls
we run and and scream and fight monsters
in the cement towers of the bronx span
we want to ascend the spooky staircase
and explore the walkway to manhattan
but mommy herds us to the playground on randall's island
where she can sit in the shade and talk to the matron
while the cars whirl overhead
and harry sits on his hill
a small patch of grass bordered by an access ramp
beneath the grand junction
where the harlem span meets the viaduct
harry in his undershirt
drinking his quart of beer hidden in a brown paper bag
basking in the sun and alone in the quiet
he does not build bridges
he does not have a car
he works hard and dies in poverty
they give his ashes to the winds
and he intersects
with everywhere in the great universe
as cars speed by
and the commuters take no notice

astoria park

the memorial is a tombstone
gray as war
gray as the hell gate's insane tides
gray as the triborough's symmetry
gray as the psychiatric hospital's lobotomized windows
gray as the railroad's commerce
gray as the skyline of the glorious city
gray as the storm we watched
father and son from the concrete bleachers
the crowd ran from the pool
raindrops splashed on the chlorine
we sat in the gray rain
we sat together

the dead are not buried here
they are gone as are the dolphins
which led the dutchman up this strait
intoxication and shipwreck
visions of the devil dancing on his stones
new amsterdam is gone
the indians are gone
this east river is toxic
it flows north and south
it never was a river
daddy tells stories of sunken treasure ships
we will never be rich
we will never be but what we are

father and son
forever in the gray rain
with our pot bellies and our pale skin
and our tender feet and our anxieties
our lifetimes of work and responsibility
maybe the car window is open

maybe the apartment is burning down
maybe the boss does not like us
and we will be sucked into homeless poverty
like locker keys into hungry drains beneath waveless waters
our possessions lost in bureaucracy
in america where the rivers are poison
and there are no free swims

this pool was built for the huddled masses
doff those work clothes and be free
bathing suit naked
beneath the lightning before the wind
in a distant memory of childhood
the iron bars keep us safe
we will not walk into the wine dark tides
of the hell gate and never return
we simply do not leave
at night underwater lights shine
like the new jerusalem
the gray sky darkens with stars
the spirit rises over radiant water

we simply will not leave

the banks of brook avenue

and brook avenue runs
straight through the crooked world
from railroad yard
north to the meat market
and curves and disappears
into the heart of the bronx
where tenements burn and die
and stare black eyed and hollow
like the dead waiting for the soul to rise
and america flies to the moon
and america drops bombs
and america makes war on crime and drugs
but brook avenue never ends
the old mill stream flows long buried
in the great sewer beneath the great street
of the great borough of the bronx
where founding fathers sleep
beneath the shadows of saint ann's church
and indian villages deconstruct
beneath abandoned factories
and the belgian paving stones on which horses clopped
lie beneath the asphalt where automobiles drift
from the bronx kill to the american mainland
and the millbrook housing projects rise to the heavens
above tarpaper roofs where pigeons and junkies
forget their way home
and the brook babbles beneath the surface
and the brook finds its way through the underworld
to the ocean that brings
immigrants to the new continent
they build skyscrapers and railroads
they fight wars and they play baseball
they make money and move to the grand concourse
they make more money and move to the suburbs

or they remain impoverished and searching
for brook avenue grass for brook avenue women
for a steady man for a steady job
for the ship that sails to paradise
the winters are cold in unheated apartments
fire hydrants flood the summer streets with toddlers
and on the banks of brook avenue i see
the world as it is
and the sun beats down
and the bootblacks toil and sweat drops from their brows
and the bootblacks beat beauty into old shoes
and the bootblacks earn a living one dollar at a time
in america where we vote for our kings
and the police beat whom they wish
and the strong beat the weak
and the women walk to store to church to playground
and the children play beneath shady tenements
where boughs of streetlights
do not dance in the wind
and the children laugh and the children cry
on the banks of brook avenue
and the sun sets and the night rises
and the pool hall grows smoky and serious
and the children dream and the children have nightmares
and the darkness of heaven and the darkness of civilization
and the sighs of the lonely and the sighs of lovers
are indistinguishable
on the banks of brook avenue
where childhood is idyllic
and the world could not be more beautiful

Bibliography: Previous Publications

avenue b, 14th street, looking south
You Are Here: New York City Streets in Poetry. P & Q Press. 2006.
Z Miscellaneous. Winter 1989.

the beach beneath the bridge
North Coast Review. Issue 7, 1995.

the fountain of youth
The Prose Poem: An International Journal. Vol. 2, 1993.

the gambling leaguers
The Glacier Stopped Here: an anthology of poems by Dane County writers. Dane County Cultural Affairs Commission & Isthmus Publishing. 1994.

grandfather: a photograph
The Spirit That Moves Us. Vol. 6, no. 1, 1981.

justice
Live Lines: Is There a Place for Poetry in Your World? Pearson Canada Inc. 2011.
And Justice For All. Perfection Learning Company. 2000.
Welcome to Your Life: Writings for the Heart of Young America. Milkweed Editions. 1998.

lost again on old subways
Tokens: Contemporary Poetry of the Subway. P & Q Press. 2003.

***ne cede malis:* poem for the seal of the borough of the bronx**
The Bronx County Historical Society Journal. Vol. XLV, nos. 1 & 2, spring/fall 2008.

on the coping
Dusty Dog. Vol. 2, no. 1, January 1991.

standing upon the fordham road bridge
Connections: New York City Bridges in Poetry. P & Q Press. 2012.
North Coast Review. Issue 7, 1995.

triborough bridge: suspension
POETS on the line. No. 3, spring 1996.

yankee kitchen
This is an elaboration of a short poem, **genghis khan,** which appeared in *Wormwood Review.* Vol. 33, no. 3, 1993.

www.ingramcontent.com/pod-product-compliance
Lightning Source LLC
Chambersburg PA
CBHW070938160426
43193CB00011B/1736